TODD PARR

TIME FOR SCHOOL ACTIVITY BOOK

LITTLE, BROWN & COMPANY
LB kids

About This Book

The art for this book was created on a drawing tablet using an iMac, starting with bold black lines and dropping in color with Adobe Photoshop. | This book was edited by Samantha Schutz and designed by Christine Kettner. | The production was supervised by Bernadette Flinn, and the production editor was Marisa Finkelstein. | The text was set in Todd Parr Regular, and the display type was hand-lettered by Todd Parr.

TODD TIME!

Hi! I'm Todd Parr, and I am the author and illustrator of this book. I put special Todd Time boxes, like this one, throughout your book. These boxes have special messages from me to YOU. Have fun!

Love, Todd

CONTENTS

THIS IS ME!

Draw yourself and don't forget to add all the details that make you YOU!

My name is

_____.

TODD TIME!

I like to paint, draw, and read. My favorite food is mac and cheese.

MY BIRTHDAY

How old are you? Circle the number.

1 2 3 4 5 6 7 8 9 10

When is your birthday?
Circle the month and day.

January   February   March   April

May   June   July   August   September

October   November   December

1	2	3	4	5	6	7	8	9	10	11	12
13	14	15	16	17	18	19	20	21	22
23	24	25	26	27	28	29	30	31

Draw the number
of candles you will need
on your next birthday cake.

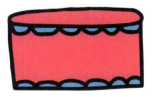

Make a wish! What did you wish for?

_____

SPECIAL

Draw your family in the picture frames.
Write their names, too.

PEOPLE

Draw your friends in the picture frames.
Write their names, too.

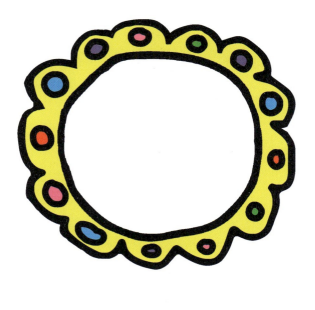

_____

_____

_____

_____

FAMILY FUN

How many members are there in each family?
Connect the picture to the number,
then color in all the pictures.

NO ONE LIKE YOU!

Can you find the two people that are the same on this page?

You're right! No one on this page is the same. Everyone is different and everyone is great—including YOU!

MY FAVORITE COLOR

Trace each word, then draw something with that color in the box.

red

orange

yellow

green

blue

purple

pink   brown   black

white

My favorite color is

_____.

My favorite color is blue. I live in a blue house, have a blue dog, and like blue pizza.

13

MY PET PAL

Do you have a pet?
If not, use your imagination. Draw it here.

What is your pet's name?

_____

PERFECT PETS

Which animals do you think would make a good pet? Draw a smiley face next to them.

Which animals do you think would not make a good pet? Draw a frowny face next to them.

DESIGN TIME

Create an outfit for this chicken. Don't forget to draw underwear on the chicken's head.

FUN TIMES

What activities do you like to do for fun? Trace each word, then **color** in your favorite activities.

playing outside

skateboarding

reading

swimming

building

HOW DO YOU FEEL?

Trace each word, then circle the words that describe how you feel today.

sad

happy

silly

scared

angry

How else do you feel?

_____

DRAW YOUR FEELINGS

What makes you feel happy?

What makes you feel angry?

What makes you feel sad?

What makes you feel silly?

ANIMAL ALPHABET

Draw a line to connect the animal
to the letter it starts with.

K

B

F

E

D

WHAT MAKES YOU FEEL GOOD?

Draw a line from each word to the matching picture.

playing

family

reading

doggy kisses

hugs

KINDNESS COUNTS

Kindness makes everyone feel good.
Trace the words, then **color** in your favorite ways to be kind.

sharing

being together

caring for plants

listening

SUPER ME!

A hero is someone who is looked up to by others.
Some heroes are famous. Others are people you see every day.
Take a look at the words in the box below.
These words describe what makes someone a hero.

brave	bold	selfless	hardworking	
strong	smart	kind	hopeful	giving
sharing	caring	loyal	helpful	loving

Who do you think is a hero? _____

Circle the words in the box that make YOU a hero.

brave	bold	selfless	hardworking	
strong	smart	kind	hopeful	giving
sharing	caring	loyal	helpful	loving

GOOD JOB!

Put a heart 💙 next to the actions that make you feel proud of yourself. I feel proud of myself when I...

...am kind. ___

...share toys. ___

...try again after
a mistake. ___

...clean my room. ___

...try a new food. ___

...listen to instructions. ___

...am gentle with people
and animals. ___

...treat the earth
with respect. ___

DON'T USE THIS PAGE!

Just kidding. Draw anything you want here.

THE FIVE SENSES

Your senses help you experience the world. Trace each word, then **color** the pictures.

see

hear

smell

taste

touch

GLASSES HELP ME SEE

Decorate the glasses.

SO MANY SMELLS

What do you think smells good? Draw a triangle around it. △

What do you think smells bad? Draw a rectangle around it. ▭

TODD TIME!

My favorite smell is wet dog.

TASTY TREATS

What are your favorite foods?
Trace each word.
Then **color** in the foods you like.

eggs

ice cream

taco

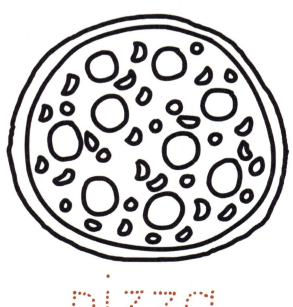

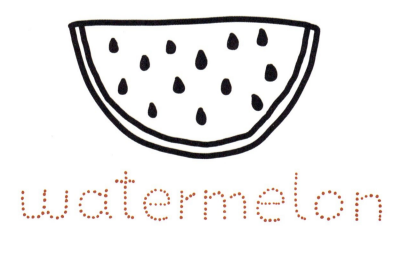

pizza

watermelon

PLAY WITH YOUR FOOD

Count the number of fruits and vegetables
in each line. Then write the number in each box.

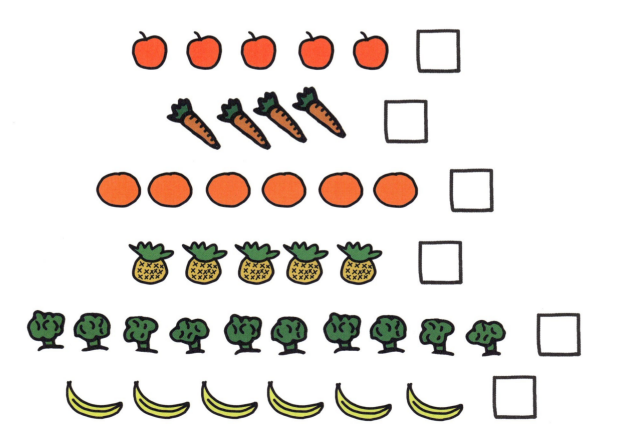

TOUCH AND FEEL

Draw a line to connect the picture to the matching word.

soft

bumpy

furry

slimy

sticky

prickly

LISTEN UP!

Connect the animal to the sound it makes.

chirp

woof

meow

roar

gurgle

buzz

hoot

hiss

quack

THE BEST TIME

The best time to eat
macaroni and cheese in the bathtub is at 2:00 PM.
Trace the time on each clock.
Then circle the clock that says 2:00 PM.

9:00 AM   2:00 PM   5:00 AM   6:00 PM

4:00 AM   1:00 PM   11:00 AM   8:00 PM

OTHER TIMES

What time do you...

...wake up?

...read?

...eat lunch?

...dance?

...play?

...go to bed?

...take a bath?

TODD TIME!

The best part of my day is when I draw pictures.

SWEET DREAMS

What is the dog dreaming about?

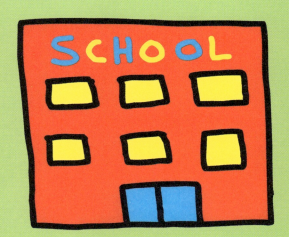

MY TOWN

Your town:

_____

Your school:

_____

What makes your neighborhood special?

_____

Draw your favorite place in your neighborhood.

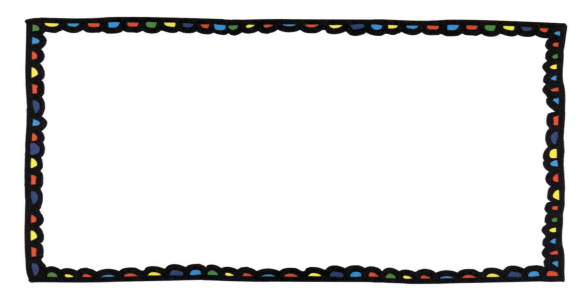

HELPERS HELP

There are so many helpers in your community.
Match each helper with the things
they use at work.

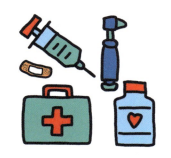

NEIGHBORS BY

There are so many things to count at this party. Fill in the answers below. Don't forget to cross each item off as you count it.

How many neighbors...

...are wearing yellow? _____

...are wearing pink? _____

...are wearing orange? _____

...are wearing purple? _____

How many balloons...

...are yellow? _____

...are pink? _____

...are orange? _____

...are purple? _____

THE NUMBERS

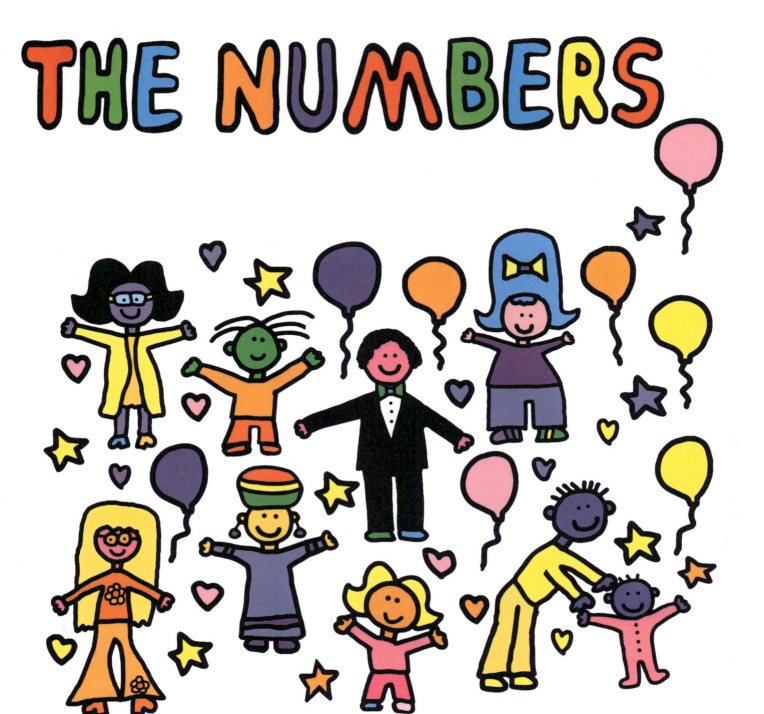

How many hearts...

...are yellow? _____

...are pink? _____

...are orange? _____

...are purple? _____

How many stars...

...are yellow? _____

...are pink? _____

...are orange? _____

...are purple? _____

LET'S GO SHOPPING

It's time to go to the supermarket. Trace each word on the shopping list, then draw a line to connect it to the matching picture.

cat food

light bulb

milk

grapes

taco

cake

watermelon

pizza

soap

macaroni and cheese

flowers

toilet paper

AT THE LIBRARY

Count the brown books. How many are there? ____
Count the kids. How many are there? ____

Can you find a heart, peace sign, and pig?
Draw a circle around each one.

TODD TIME!

I love to read books about space.

45

BUBBLE TROUBLE

It's laundry day and there are bubbles floating all over the laundromat. Color in the bubbles according to the color key.

red 1   orange 2   yellow 3

green 4   blue 5   pink 6   purple 7

SHAPE SCHOOL

Count the shapes in each line.
Then write the number in each box.

TRUCKS AROUND TOWN

There are a lot of trucks on the road today.
These trucks are making patterns! Complete each pattern
by finding the correct sticker on your sticker sheet.

AT THE PARK

Who is at the park today?
Draw or use your stickers to finish the scene.

VISIT TO THE DOCTOR

It's time for a checkup at the doctor.
The doctor needs to look at your EYES, listen
to your HEART and LUNGS, and look inside your
EARS, MOUTH, and NOSE. Can you find those six
words hidden in the puzzle below?

```
H E A R T M L
N S W V J F U
N O S E V E N
S V R K A Y G
E A R S E E S
S M N Z L S O
I M O U T H W
```

PIZZA PARTY

How many slices of pizza are there? _____

How many pepperonis are on the pizza? _____

What are your favorite pizza toppings?
Draw them on the pizza.

TODD TIME!

My favorite pizza topping is worms.

DANCE PARTY

Fill this page with people dancing.

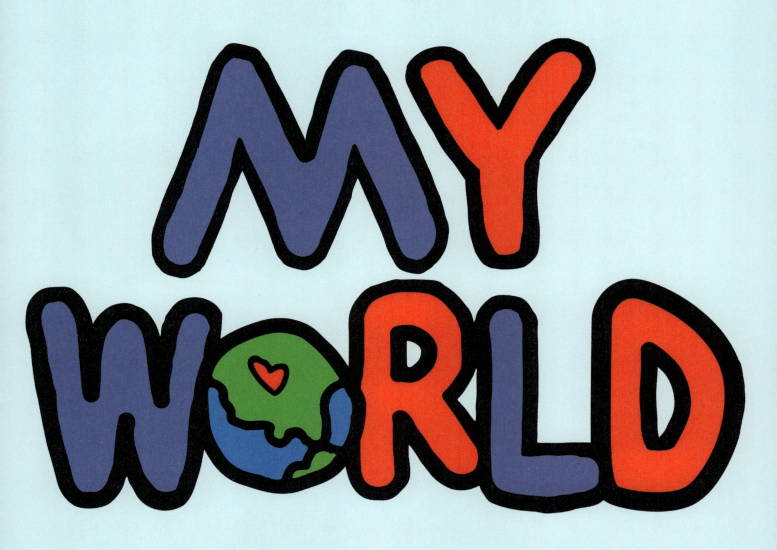

PICK A PLANET

Circle the earth in each row
that is different.

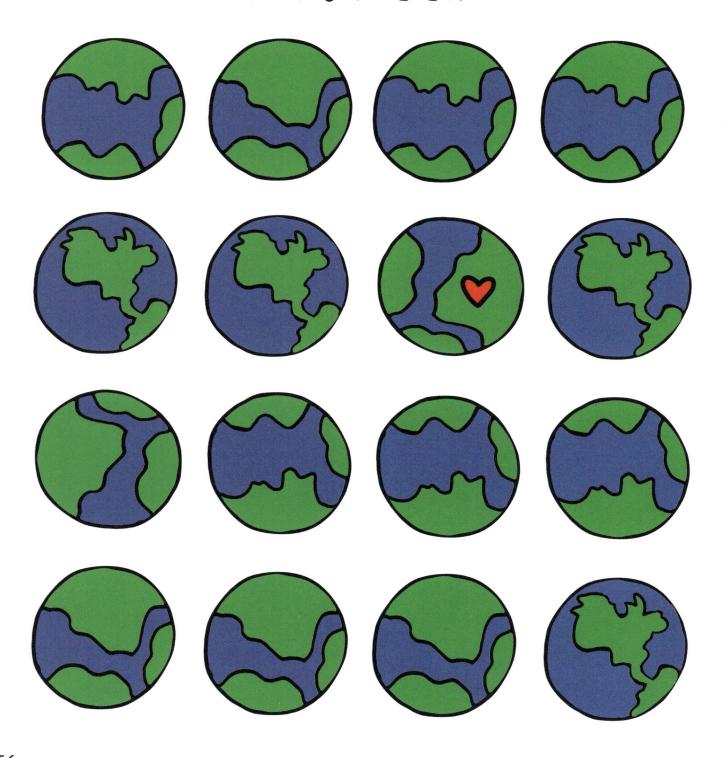

HELP THE EARTH

Check out these ways to be kind to the earth.

Walk, bike, carpool, or take the bus to get where you are going. This reduces air pollution.

Recycle, so trash can be transformed into new things.

RECYCLE GLASS

TRASH

Turn off the sink and lights when you're not using them. That saves water and energy.

Plant a tree to create shade and keep the air clean.

Can you think of any other ways to be kind to the earth?

_____

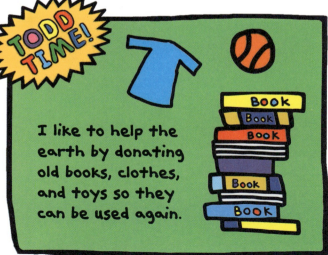

TODD TIME!

I like to help the earth by donating old books, clothes, and toys so they can be used again.

TURN THIS PAGE UPSIDE DOWN!

There are no rules here.
Do whatever you want with this page.

WHAT'S THE WEATHER?

Place a sunshine sticker next to the warm-weather clothes.

Place a snowflake sticker next to the cold-weather clothes.

CHILLY CODE

Use the code to reveal a secret message.

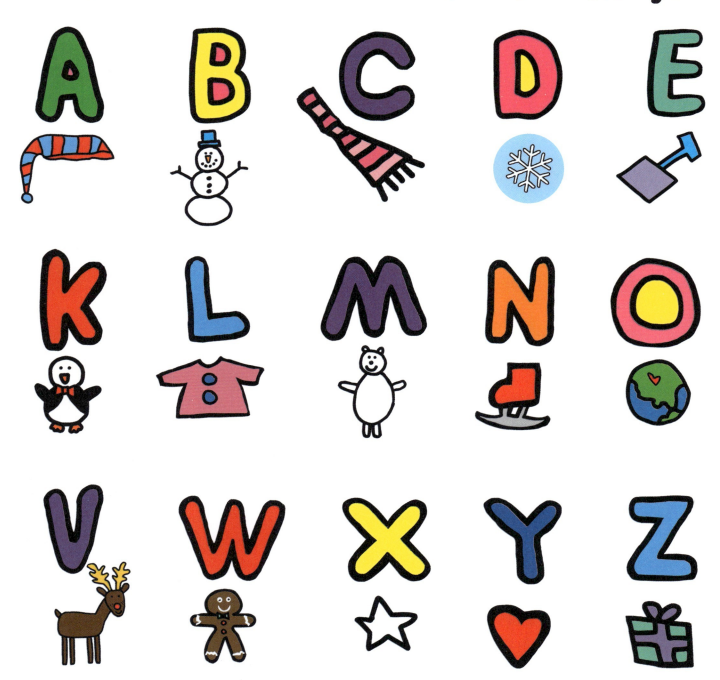

F G H I J

P Q R S T U

WHAT'S DIFFERENT?

Spot the seven differences in each pair.

SPRING SHOWERS

IT'S RAINING!
The letters in the word **RAIN** are hidden in the raindrops. Can you find each letter and then color in that raindrop?

SPRING FLOWERS

Color the first flower **RED**. Color the second flower **YELLOW**.
Color the third flower **PINK**. Color the fourth flower **PURPLE**.

Which color flower is the tallest? _____

Which color flower is the shortest? _____

Which color flower has the most petals? _____

Which color flower has the fewest petals? _____

SUMMER SUN

Trace the words, then color your favorite summer activities.

TODD TIME!

My favorite thing about summer is the fireflies.

MERMAID MYSTERY

Use the code to reveal the answer to the joke.

HOW MANY LEAVES?

Count the leaves in each line.
Then write the number in each box.

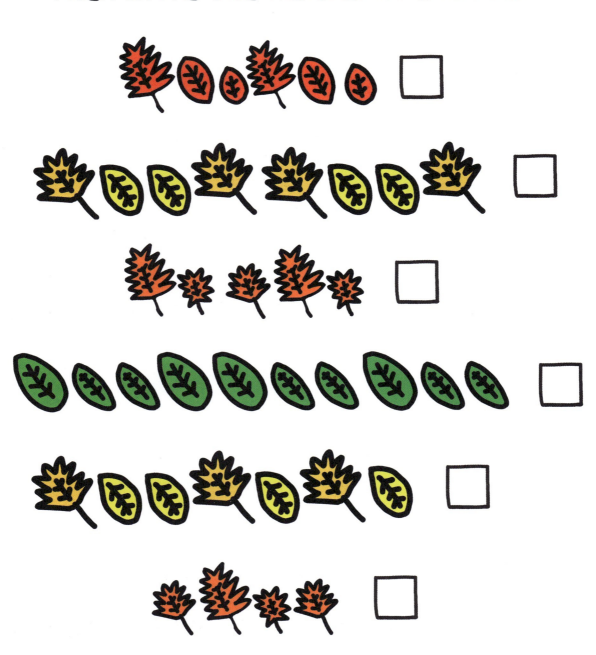

WINDY DAY!

The fall wind blew all the leaves around. Can you find
the letters that spell **AUTUMN**?
Then **color** in those leaves.

TAKE A TRIP!

Ready to take a vacation? You've got to pack your suitcase first. Draw a square ▢ around the things you might need for your trip. Draw a circle ⃝ around the things you won't need.

UNDER THE WAVES

Draw things that live in the ocean.

TODD TIME!

I love swimming. Add me to your drawing.

WHICH WAY?

How many fish are swimming to the left? ____

How many fish are swimming to the right? ____

Circle the fish that are swimming up.

Put a square around the fish that are swimming down.

Which direction is the yellow fish facing? ____

Give the purple fish a name. _____

PENGUIN PARTY

Circle the two penguins that are the same.

AT THE FARM

Count the animals, then write the number of animals in the box above each image. Add up the number of animals to get the total.

UP IN THE AIR

Draw things that fly in the sky.

SPACED OUT

Draw a scene from space.

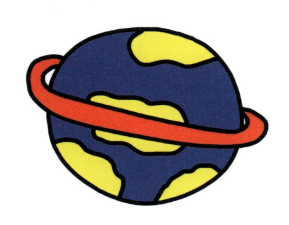

MAKE A WISH!

Write or draw your wish inside the star.
Then color this page.

ANSWER KEY

Page 10

Page 20
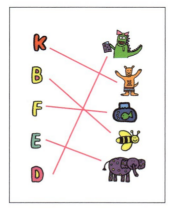

Page 21
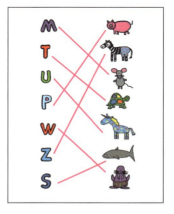

Page 22
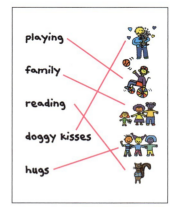

Page 31
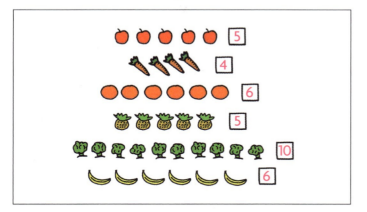

Page 32

Page 33

Page 34

Page 41

Page 42

How many neighbors...

...are wearing yellow? 4
...are wearing pink? 5
...are wearing orange? 3
...are wearing purple? 4

How many balloons...

...are yellow? 3
...are pink? 5
...are orange? 3
...are purple? 3

Page 43

How many hearts...

...are yellow? 5
...are pink? 7
...are orange? 4
...are purple? 5

How many stars...

...are yellow? 7
...are pink? 1
...are orange? 5
...are purple? 4

Page 44

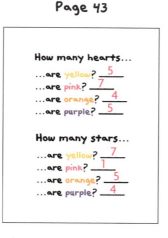

cat food
light bulb
milk
grapes
taco
cake
watermelon
pizza
soap
macaroni and cheese
flowers
toilet paper

Page 45

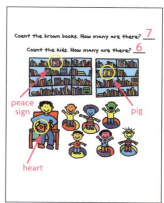

Count the brown books. How many are there? 7

Count the kids. How many are there? 6

peace sign
pig
heart

Page 46

Page 47

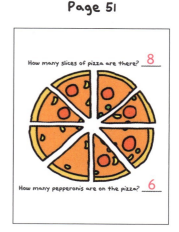

6
4
8
7
8
13

Page 48

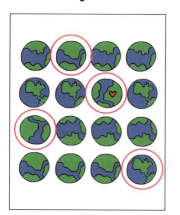

Page 50

Page 51

How many slices of pizza are there? 8

How many pepperonis are on the pizza? 6

Page 56

Page 59

Page 61

S P R E A D
L O V E
A N D J O Y !

Page 62

Page 63

Page 64

Which color flower is the tallest? __red__

Which color flower is the shortest? __yellow__

Which color flower has the most petals? __yellow__

Which color flower has the fewest petals? __pink__

Page 67

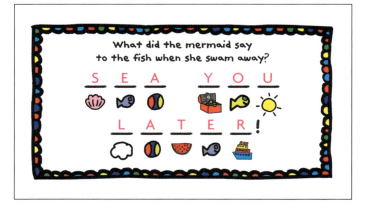

What did the mermaid say to the fish when she swam away?

S E A   Y O U   L A T E R !

Page 68

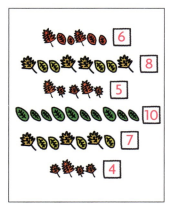

Page 69

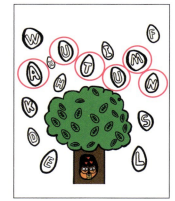

Page 72

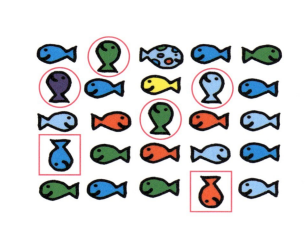

How many fish are swimming to the left? __14__

How many fish are swimming to the right? __5__

Which direction is the yellow fish facing? __left__

Page 73

Page 74

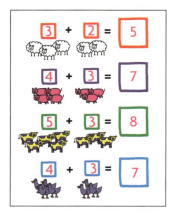

3 + 2 = 5

4 + 3 = 7

5 + 3 = 8

4 + 3 = 7